SOME ANGELS
SPEAK FRENCH

Otto Baruch Rand

I would like to thank Pia Aitken and Mel Goldberg for their work in editing. Thank you also to Sheila Turner for reading and commenting on this manuscript.

Too many books about this period of time recount only the horrors. This book recounts the courage of some wonderful people of Slovakia, who cared for my family during those terrible times.

ISBN-10: 1974544613
ISBN-13: 978-1974544615

DEDICATION

I dedicate this book to the heroine of my life, my mother, Leah Rosalia Rand, for her heroic behavior in saving our lives.

CHAPTER ONE:
BRUSHED BY DEATH

January, 1945

Our young mother stares down at us, her two sons, Ernest and Otto, lying in the snow, as the last remaining reservoirs of her strength slowly, and visibly, drains away. Her sunken eyes are infinitely deep wells of sadness, but her voice is resolute.

"This is the point of our deaths. We are too cold. We have no food or strength left. We cannot go on. Since you were born, I have loved you with all my heart, as I loved your father. Now, before we lie down to a final sleep, I will give you the blessing given to our fathers and mothers and to all the generations before them when they were dying."

She removes her gloves and places worn hands, blue with cold, on each child's head, and chants the most holy of all Jewish prayers: *"Shma, Yisrael, Adonai Eloheynu, Adonai Echad."*

Tears freeze on her eyelashes before they can run down her face. She tucks their warm hats around their faces, puts her gloves back on, and curls her body around her youngest son, Ernest. They both fall asleep instantly.

Our walk through the knee-deep-to-an-adult snow in the pathless forest after our narrow midnight escape from the Nazi Hlinka Guard had completely exhausted us.

Until our forest escape, we had been hiding in the apartment of Mischa, a brick factory worker, who was a member of the Slovak Resistance against the Nazis. He had been recommended by Janicek, our contact person with the Slovak Resistance. Mischa's little house, located in a complex built for the factory workers, had two bedrooms. Rosalia and we two boys occupied one bedroom. Mischa and his wife had the other one. My mother was an attractive woman and although Misha was a very kind and respectable man, he paid more attention to her than he should have, which she did not reciprocate. Misha's wife was jealous. A heavy drinker, she spent many of her evenings in local taverns. Although warned by her husband never tell anyone about their "guests," when she was drunk, which happened frequently, her jealousy and wine loosened her tongue.

One evening in January, when Misha sat in the living room with my mother and us showing us the weapons the

3

Resistance deposited in his house, we heard an unexpected knock on the door. Misha threw the gun and the revolvers out of the window and they disappeared in the deep snow that had covered the ground that month, the coldest and snowiest of the year . Then came another knock, harder and louder. When Misha opened the door, three Hlinka Gardists entered the house dressed in their official black uniforms.They asked for everyone's identifications. Misha pulled out his identification, but their eyes were focused at Rosalia. Slowly she pulled out from her handbag her fake identification, showing that she was a Slovak woman from the east of the country. But the Gardists knew.

The one who seemed to be the commander said, "This is not your real identity. You are Jews." For a minute, we were all silent. "So take whatever you can and come with us. We must send you where all Jews are being sent."

At this moment seven-year-old Ernest burst in tears. "Please, don't take us away. We are good people, We never did anything wrong to anyone."

The older Guardist was somewhat surprised and moved. "No, we will not take you. Only your mother."

At this moment Ernest fell to the ground and hugged the legs of the Guardist. "No, please, we are small. We cannot survive without our mother!"

There was some softening in the face of the commander, who was Slovak and not a Nazi. He called his companions to a corner for consultation. Then he came forward and announced firmly, "We must take you. These are our orders. But we will allow you a few hours to pack your belongings. We will be back early in the morning." Then they exited the house and we all felt relief.

"They gave us a chance to escape," said Rosalia, "but where can we go?"

"There is a village, Maluzina, some 25 kilometrers east of here," said Misha, "which is still in the hands of the resistance. But there is no road there. You can get there only through the mountains and it's very cold and the snow is very high. You will never make it."

"If the choice is between being taken to a concentration camp and a nearly impossible chance to escape, we take the escape option," said our mother.

She dressed us as warmly as she could, with two sweaters and two pairs of socks, tucked in woolen boots which reached above our knees. She hastily baked hot dumplings and took some cheese from the refrigerator. Fortunately, Misha's wife was not yet at home so we quickly left and started off in the direction of Maluzina. Since there was no road, we simply followed our instinct. I looked around in the starry night and tried to discover some path. All I could see were some telephone lines, so I said, "Telephone lines must lead to an inhabited place. Let us follow them." My mother and Ernest agreed.

Our progress was very slow, since it was very hard, particularly for small Ernest, who had to pull his little legs out of deep snow at every step, but we moved ahead, all the time following the telephone lines. We walked slower and slower for five hours, but we found no village.

Unfortunately, we had eaten the dumplings and cheese my mother had hurriedly prepared in the hour before we started our trek up the mountain. There was no water but we had snow. At about 4:30 AM, the temperature had dropped to 20 degrees below zero. When we found a rock clearing, we decided to rest. That was when Ernest and our mother fell deeply asleep.

But I was only ten years old and fearful that we would end up being some bear's dinner so I could not sleep. I had read a book about bears awaking in mid-winter and wandering about looking for food after their long hibernation. For several minutes, I lay awake, attentive to sounds around me. Besides my fear of bears my feet were so cold they hurt. I moved a short distance away from my mother and brother, took off my boots and rubbed my feet until I could feel my toes again. A few minutes later, I heard the crunching of footsteps in the snow. It was so pitch dark in the forest that I could see almost nothing.

"Hey, who is there?" I shouted, suppressing my fear that it would be bears who didn't speak Slovak.

Fortunately there were no bears, just two partisans who spoke very bad Slovak with a French accent.

"What are you doing here?" they asked.

"We are on our way to Maluzina. We are resting because my little brother couldn't walk any further," I replied.

"We?" asked the man, puzzled.

"My mother and brother are sleeping over there," I said, pointing to their rock-bed a couple of yards away. "We just barely escaped the Hlinka Guard after we were denounced by the woman where we were staying. We have walked all night across the mountain, following the telephone lines."

"You cannot stay here," one said. "You will die from the cold. Maluzina is only one hour away walking, so you must continue and not stop."

I stood up. I could still feel my feet and toes when I moved them. I thought I could walk. But neither my brother nor my mother had wakened during the whole conversation.

The two men walked to them and shook them, but they didn't respond. The men removed two flasks of cognac from their heavy coats. They dripped a little down the throats of my mother and brother, who wakened violently as they choked on the stinging heat of the burning liquid.

One of the men pulled my mother to her feet and instructed her clearly and rather harshly, "You cannot stay here and rest. You will all freeze to death. You must get on your feet and move on. It is only one more hour of walking until you are in Maluzina. You can make it. This boy can lead you," he said, pointing to me. "I have told him to continue following the phone lines and follow our footsteps. Now go!"

The French partisans disappeared into the snowy darkness. I was grateful that even in the deepest darkness, if there is snow, there is some small light to enable us to see phone lines. *But follow their footsteps? Doubtful*, I thought.

I suspected my mother and Ernest had frostbitten toes, which made walking very–difficult for them. Ernest had to raise his legs very high to forge a path through snow which was up to his hips and still falling.

After two hours, we saw no town, but discovered a small gazebo ahead of us in the snowy pre-dawn mist. Though the sides were open, it had a roof and benches so it provided some shelter. Best of all, it was an indication of civilization nearby. In the distance, we could hear the sounds of warfare, guns and cannons. When dawn broke, we were able to see a house about 300 meters away.

We knocked on the door of the rather large house which was opened by a local forester and his wife who greeted us warmly. "Come in quickly," the wife said, peering nervously left and right outside the door before she closed it behind us.

She looked at our pitiful little group, dripping with icicles, which told her everything. "Quickly, take off your pants and shoes and socks," she said as she poured warm water into a tub. "Put your feet in here. We must prevent frostbite."

My shoes and socks came off easily, and the tub of water in the warm house felt like paradise.

But my mother and Ernest could not get their boots off. Their feet had frozen inside them. The wife made a second tub of lukewarm water with salt. Feet and boots went in together. It took hours, but finally the boots came off. All the toes on

Ernest's right foot were black. My mother had only eight toes undamaged by frostbite.

Later, as we sat down to eat a generous breakfast prepared by the forester's wife, four other couples emerged from bedrooms above, asking many questions.

"Where have you come from? Why were you walking through the forest at night? Where is your father?"

"We walked here from Mikulash," I answered.

"That is not possible," replied the astonished forester. "It is 25 kilometers and way below freezing. There is no road. How . . . ? "

"It's true," my mother said, interrupting him. "God helped us. God saved us."

But my thoughts disputed my mother's assessment. *No, mother,* I said silently to myself, *Not God, the French partisans.*

"We came to Maluzina," I explained, "because your village is in the hands of the Resistance."

"No more," the forester said ominously, "no more. This morning they were chased out by a Ukranian-Nazi unit of Vlasov. So now we are back in the hands of the Nazis. They are camped just on the other side of the village. We are all in serious danger. And we have no more rooms. There are already four couples of refugees in our house. You cannot stay here."

I looked at my mother, wondering how much more she and Ernest could take. *Displaced again,* I thought, *just when we had fought so hard to get to a place we believed was safe? Where could we go now?*

CHAPTER TWO:
AN UNFORGETTABLE DAY

March 27, 1942

The day dawned cold and damp, welcomed only by a wet, slow, drizzling rain. To my surprise, I wakened to hear my parents arguing in the next room. I had never heard them fight before, so I crept to the door to listen.

"You have to be realistic, Mano," I heard my mother say to my father very firmly. "You think the Germans are a rational people, but they aren't at the moment. They elected Hitler, after all."

"Lenke, these are the people of Beethoven and Goethe. They are not uncivilized Goths. Be reasonable!" he replied, sounding very irritated.

"Please, PLEASE, Mano." She began crying. "You are my beloved husband and the only father our boys have. If anything happens to you, I won't know what to do without you. It's bad enough that the Nazis have stolen your barber shop and beauty salon so we have no income . . . but to lose you, too . . . "

"You are NOT going to lose me, Lenke. I'm going to a work camp. The Germans need workers for the war effort. It makes sense. Why would they kill able-bodied men when they need workers? Oh, my Lenke, my beautiful wife . . . "

Then their voices became silent. I crept out into the kitchen and looked longingly at the counter where the metal bread box stood almost empty. My mother had always kept it full of delicious breads and cakes and let my father, brother, and me help ourselves. But lately, flour was in short supply, and butter was almost non-existent. Jews were forced to walk a very long way to get groceries at a store that often didn't have much. So there was very little bread in the box. I took nothing, knowing my mother would be rationing the little bit there for our breakfast.

I tiptoed back to the bedroom that I shared with my younger brother, Ernest, who was only five. My parents had always encouraged me to read books on science and nature so I sat down on the bed and picked up the book I had been reading about bears.   After we had shared a meager breakfast of bread, cheese, and tea set out by my mother, she dressed us warmly for a carriage ride. Normally, my brother and I would have been very excited. We loved carriage rides. But this day, the mood was gloomy. My father seemed firm in his decision. He was reserved, and determined but my mother shook her head, distraught.

Over and over, during the ride, she pleaded with my father not to go. "Please, please, my beloved, we can go immediately to Mikulash in the east. My family is still there. They are not collecting Jews there, at least not yet. We can live with them. Please, Mano." Tears were running down her cheeks again.

"Lenke, running from the Hlinka Guard is a very risky business. They have sent me orders to appear." he said. "Now look. It is settled. I'm going today, but I will be back soon, you will see."

Ernest and I tuned out the bitterness coming from the front seat by playing a game in the back. At the time I wondered how anything could be that serious? Besides, I couldn't wait to see the beautiful train cars again. Every summer, our family had traveled by train to see our grandmother in Mikulash. We sat in the red-carpeted, comfortable cars leaning against big, wood-framed windows watching the world fly by. Now my father was going to ride in one. How lovely it would be. I was even a little jealous.

My attitude changed when we reached the station. The horses came to a stop in a line of other carriages. We got down and entered the station building but when I looked out the door to where the tracks were I saw no familiar trains meant for people. The only cars I could see in the distance were very old, run-down box-cars with giant sliding doors, the type of cars used to haul cattle. I did not understand what was going on? Many Jews were waiting in line at the station to board. One of them came over to my father, Emanuel, and said they were all going to be loaded onto that cattle train. I did not believe him and decided to check for myself.

I opened the station door leading to the tracks and ran toward the train, as my parents shouted for me to come back, their voices receding into the background as I got closer and closer to the train. I jumped over the tracks and peered into the door of the first car. There were no seats, only an empty and dirty train car with single slats of wood for a floor and cracks in the walls. Instantly, I knew something was very wrong!

A tall man in a green uniform shouted at me. "Hey, kid, get away from there."

But I was fast. In no time I was back in the station. "Daddy," I said, "listen to Mama. Do not go. This is not right. This is not a train for people. It is for cattle. You do not belong on it. There is a mistake. Mama is right, Daddy!"

But my father said nothing, paying absolutely no attention to my pleas. He approached the outside door of the station, kissed his wife good-bye, reached back and hugged Ernest and me, picked up his large bag and turned to walk to the end of the line. My mother saw the fear on my face, and spoke to reassure me. Somehow, her words did not match her reassuring tone. "Otto, your father always believes in obeying the law, and he has been commanded to appear, so appear he will. There is nothing we can do to stop him."

Soon, soldiers appeared and began shoving the men into the very same car I had looked into. One man stumbled trying to climb the high step, and my father reached down to pull him up. As he stood back up, he waved toward us. Before we could wave back, he had already disappeared inside the boxcar.

Then Mother looked down. Near her feet was her husband's smaller bag containing his underwear and toothbrush. She opened the door and began running toward the train, shouting for the soldiers to wait. As they closed the door on the men crammed inside, she reached the first guard. "Please, please give this to my husband. It's his underwear. He forgot it," she begged.

The soldier reached out, snatched the bag from my mother and pitched it over the railroad tracks where it fell open, spilling the contents onto the damp earth. "Get lost, lady," he said as he spun around and pulled himself up to a narrow platform at the end of the car.

My mother stood there, momentarily unable to move.

I watched, horrified. My strong, wise father had just disappeared into a cattle car filled with most of the Jewish men from our small town of Piestany, founded a century earlier. Piestany was a town in which some Jews had developed spa hotels and restaurants for visitors who came to "take the waters" for healing and comfort. All these town stalwarts had seen their businesses plundered and taken by gentiles in the previous six months before they had been taken away. Now they themselves had been squeezed as if they were

15

non-human forms in a moving hovel which was slowly pulling away from the town station.

Even little Ernest seemed to understand the implications, if not the magnitude, of the calamity we were witnessing. He started to cry. "Where did they take *Apo*? I'm afraid. Where is *Apush*?" But there was no answer to his anguished question.

Rosalia gathered her natural, formidable presence about herself, lifted her long gray skirt slightly over her black stockings and worn shoes, and walked back into the station. She spoke not a word - perhaps unable to talk without weeping. Inside, the warmth of human bodies barely dispelled the chill of dispirited souls. A few wives of some of the Jewish men who had been taken had made onion soup in one house. All were sharing the soup, but Ernest took one taste and pushed it away. I also spit it out. Our mother's dishwater would have tasted better, although she protested that we should eat.

Riding in a carriage was not something our mother did often. Half-way home, she asked the coachman to pull the carriage up to the house of some friends, the Kaufmans. "I'm stopping to see if Aliza might have a few eggs we could borrow," she explained as she climbed down. "Please stay in your seats, boys. I'm coming right back."

I was sitting in the front next to the coachman and begged to be allowed to drive the horses. The coachman did not pay attention to my request.

After two knocks at the Kaufman's door with no response, Rosalia returned to the carriage. "We will have potato soup for supper tonight," she announced stonily.

CHAPTER THREE:
CONFISCATION, ISOLATION, AND SKEPTICISM

By 1942, when my father was taken, Europe had become a seething cauldron of political intrigue and violent upheaval. History's most prolific assassin was stirring the toxic brew. The western countries, particularly England during the late 1930's, had desperately tried to avoid war. They had permitted themselves to be deceived over and over again, as Germany was busily taking over country after country either by invasion or stealth. Slovakia, where my family lived, had been taken by stealth.

Afraid of a major provocation that would pull the Allies into action in Europe, Hitler, instead of marching into Slovakia as he had into Poland and Austria, stuck his foot through Slovakia's back door. Germany made it independent of the Czech part, and installed an allied priest name Joseph

Tiso as its president. Since Germany had an alliance with Hungary, Slovakia was "officially" notified that the German government had given its approval to Hungary to annex southern Slovakia which had native Hungarians in its population, although the majority were still Slovaks.

About 1700 sq. km. of Slovak territory had been ceded to Hungary which had allied itself with Germany to avoid war. The territories annexed handed over its valuable natural resources which provided an invaluable war-time boost for Germany. The so-called peace with Hungary lasted until 1944 when Bulgaria and Romania pulled out of the Axis coalition, fueling Hitler's fears that Hungary would do the same. On March 12, 1944, he sent troops to occupy Hungary and Adolf Eichmann to institute his Final Solution for Hungarian Jews and Romas, Hungarian gypsies.

Meanwhile, the Slovakian *Final Solution* was well underway, having begun early in 1942, just before our father was taken from Piestany. Until then, I had attended a Jewish Day School which offered both Jewish and secular studies. The Nazis closed it in January and sent the all Jewish children to a school for Romas, another socially unacceptable ethnic minority. In an odd twist, the Gypsy children made fun of the Jewish children.

After a childhood which had been relatively normal, as peaceful as any life can be in a city that was populated by many Jews and free of anti-semitism, I was both puzzled and angry, well aware that what the Roma children were saying was untrue and that the gypsies themselves were victims of discrimination. I thought it was strange that they called me names.

One day after school I ran into the house, threw off my coat and sat down. "Mama, *Apo*, I must tell you about what happened at school today," I said in my breathless 9-year-old voice. "One of the Roma boys, Pavel, said I was a dirty Jew. When I said I wasn't either, he said I was a liar and that Jews are exploiters. What does that mean?"

"Well, first it means the boy is ignorant," my father responded. "Second, it means he has heard this from somebody else, because a boy your age doesn't know words like *exploiter*. And third, it means you should have reported him to your teacher."

"But *Apo*, I did. My teacher looked mad when I told him. He said I was a Jew and I must take what they say. He also said he did not want me to complain to him anymore."

The next day my mother removed me from that school and began teaching me at home. This occurred about two months before my father was taken. Education, both religious and secular, is the paramount focus in any Jewish home. Although my father, as the owner of a beauty salon and a barber shop, would not have been considered an intellectual, he was a fairly successful artisan and the grandson of the eminent and well-educated Rabbi Moises Rand from Krakow, Poland. Emanuel's father, Samuel, had not wanted to follow his Rabbi father into the Orthodox Jewish tradition, so he ran away from Krakow to Ilava in western Slovakia where Emanuel was born in 1902, the same year Rabbi Moises Rand died. Samuel, like his son after him, became the proprietor of barber shops and beauty salons.

One day in the early months of 1942, my father, Emanuel took me to a bookstore near the main square. He showed me a large map in the store's window illustrating the German advance into Austria, Poland, Holland, Yugoslavia, Belgium, France and Slovakia. With great trepidation, he described to me how the Germans were winning on their march through Europe. But I remember his reassurances again and again that our family will be fine.

"The Germans are a cultured and educated people," he said. "They are not an uncivilized people."

But even as Hitler advanced through Eastern Europe, a schism developed between eastern and western Jews. Eastern Jews were Yiddish speaking, coming from Russia and Poland. Our family, the Rands, were Western Jews, German and Hungarian speaking because, for two generations, we had lived in the Austro-Hungarian Empire. My brother and I spoke German as our first language.

"It is the language of the most cultured people in the world," Emanuel often said. "They cannot be doing what people say they are doing."

When I asked exactly what they were doing, the answers were evasive. I gathered it was that they seemed to be taking over Europe. But I wondered that if they were educated and cultured, how could that be bad.

Then I began to figure it out for myself. In the fall of 1942, before the worst had begun, a group of Hitler Youth, called the *Hitler Jugend*, came to the part of Piestany where my great-aunt lived. I often played there with friends. When I heard the new group of boys speaking German, I mingled among them and found them to be very friendly.

We all laughed and played together until somebody pulled down my pants and screamed, "He's a Jew."

At that point, the boys began hitting and kicking me until my father, who had fortunately arrived to visit his aunt, rescued me and offered a stern caution: "Never go where there are German youth. It is dangerous."

A few months after our visit to the bookstore, my father's businesses were "Aryanized." They were taken from him and given to Slovaks. One of his assistants was given the businesses, and he refused to even employ my father as a barber.

When my father appealed to him at the shop, he said, "One of the conditions of my being given this business was that I could never hire a Jew or a Roma."

The arrogant new owner, brandishing his silver razor and brown leather strop, turned his back on my father and and returned to his clients.

Emanuel remained without a job for three months until he was summoned to the "work camp." Our family had some savings that sustained us, but we obviously didn't live very well. My endlessly inventive mother, Rosalia, was always able to cook something and in addition, she sewed clothing for the family and made blankets and bedding from scraps. Although all Jewish businesses in Piestany were confiscated and in 1941 all Jews were forced to wear the Yellow Star of David and were banned from many public places, nobody had any idea of the horror that was to come. That year in Wanaee, Hitler had signed the plans for a *Final Solution* - the death of every Jew in Europe.

Nobody in this educated, German-speaking community wanted to believe it. On Friday nights after synagogue services as groups of Jews walked home together, one could hear these statements of disbelief: "My uncle in Warsaw wrote and said they tried to kill every Jew. Why would they do that? Maybe it's just the war and he thinks they are targeting Jews. Surely they would not do that sort of thing. Jews have been assimilated in Germany for generations."

But my mother, Rosalia Rand, was the skeptical voice in the crowd, much more suspicious of the Germans, possibly because she was a more practical and realistic person. Perhaps that eventually was the secret of our family's salvation.

CHAPTER FOUR:
THE FLIGHT

I loved Piestany. It was a small but elegant city world renowned for its spas, where rheumatism was treated with hot mud baths. People came to Piestany from all over the world by train and in fancy cars. Even a maharaja from India arrived once, accompanied by camels. Its fame could be seen in the parking lots of the luxurious hotels. My friends and I visited these parking lots frequently admiring the cars and imagining the wonders of the world.

Piestany had also a huge park, with many tennis courts, several golf courses, and two modern theaters. I loved the shady lanes of elm trees, the flower beds with hidden benches, and the Vah river banks lined by luxury shops and bakeries. Many times my father would take me there for ice cream or a Napoleon cake, but after his barber shops had been taken away from him, there was no money for such luxuries. Still I could not imagine living elsewhere.

Until the fateful day when everything changed, the day my father had been taken to the "work camp."

A knock had come at our apartment door in mid-afternoon in the spring of 1942. Walking confidently and unafraid down the hall, Rosalia walked past the barber shop on the first floor and opened the door to the stairs leading up from the street. Through the open door walked one of the prettiest women I had ever seen.

My mother introduced her to us. "Otto and Ernest, this is Pauline from Paris. She has come to Piestany to work as a masseuse in the spas. She will also buy our furniture."

I knew that because of the spas, there were many French citizens in Piestany. "Mama," I asked, "will we have to live without furniture?"

"No, Otto. We are leaving Piestany tomorrow morning and going to Mikulash to stay with my family, but you are not to say a word about this to anyone, do you understand?"

We boys stood in stunned silence for a moment, then I said, "Yes, Mama,"

Almost in a whisper, Ernst said, "Okay, Mama."

As the woman toured the house with my mother, I felt a clutching in my stomach. The family would be leaving this city, the only place I had ever lived. Our father had disappeared. *Obviously*, I thought, *mother must have told Apo*

*where we are going so that when he comes back he can find
us.*

But I wondered why we were leaving everything? *My
bookcases? My toy box? My own bed? Everything?*

I walked into my room and looked around, as if to
memorize every detail. I could not fathom being away from
this room. I stared at the small brown bear sitting on the
window sill, given to me when I was three by my
grandmother. I had neglected it lately, sticking it there in the
window on top of the animal stories from my earliest years.
And the little table and chair my uncle had bought for me to
use for my puzzles? White with painted white and blue
designs characteristic of western Slovakia. I hadn't thought
much about it being there. It just was. Until now, when I was
going to lose it.

We are selling our furniture to Pauline and we are
leaving, Mother had said to us. And we were to tell no one. As
if everything were hers to sell and nothing was mine. Maybe I
had no say. But were things really this bad? Maybe it wasn't.
We were going to Mikulash.

My mind whirled, twisting round and round what I had
heard, what I understood and what I didn't. *Were my uncles
and grandma in Mikulash going to be nice to us? How big was
their house? Mikulash is a long way from here, five hours by
train. What if there is nothing there to play with and I had left
all my toys behind? What if there are no books?*

I knew my mother had been distraught for the last two weeks since my father left, but perhaps she was being a little hurried in this decision? Then I remembered whispered conversations in the kitchen that weren't as quiet as the adults had thought. I heard m mother was asking friend after friend among her gentile acquaintances whom she had invited in for tea and cakes whether she and the boys could hide in their homes or if they knew anyplace else available for hiding three Jews. She had obviously been unsuccessful if we were leaving for Mikulash.

As I sat, disconsolate in my bedroom, wondering how it would feel to sleep here in my own bed for the last night, I couldn't get out of my mind the picture of my mother sobbing uncontrollably after her husband had been slammed inside the filthy cattle car. *Perhaps she did know best*, I thought. *There are worse fates than running to Mikulash without any furniture.*

When my mother and Pauline finished the house tour and agreed on a price, they returned to the kitchen where Rosalia made tea and called for us boys.

She told us that Pauline had agreed to do something very brave and dangerous.

"Boys, I have already packed your sachels and we are leaving at seven in the morning. Now there is something you must pay close attention to. It is very important. You will be traveling with Pauline as her two children. I will be dressed as a peasant woman elsewhere on the train, and you must not act as if you recognize me. If anyone asks, you cling to Pauline as your Mama, and you just say, "Mama, mama."

"No, not exactly," Pauline corrected her. "In French, it's *Maman, Maman*! Practice saying it, boys."

Dutifully, we repeated, "Maman" over and over again until she was satisfied.

"If guards appear, don't talk to them in Slovak or German. You are French children, and you speak only French, but since you don't, just say, *Maman* as if you are afraid to talk."

The next morning came too soon. I had planned to be up to say goodbye personally to each of my toys and books, but before the sun was up, my mother had pulled me from bed and helped me dress. "Come quickly to the kitchen. I have some bread and fruit for you, and then we must take the carriage to the station," she said.

I had no time for goodbyes except for a short hug of my bear. I couldn't leave it so surreptitiously, I jammed it into my satchel before taking it to the kitchen.

The journey started predictably with us boys watching the scenery fly by and counting the electrical posts, playing games spinning our heads to count. But within an hour, the Hlinka Guard appeared in our compartment. While we buried our heads in Pauline's thighs, the Guard checked her documents. Luckily for us, her passport listed her two French sons who had not come with her to Slovakia. The inspection passed quickly. The Guards were more interested in flirting with Pauline than checking her two little boys. They asked her a few questions, and it was all over. They left, sliding the door closed behind them. I breathed again but Ernst started to cry.

Pauline cuddled him close. The other passenger in the compartment didn't ask questions.

As soon as the Hlinka Guards were out of sight, I went out to the bathroom and spotted my mother in the hallway of the car watching the compartment, but I didn't say a word to her. She must have hidden in the bathroom when the Guard searched papers in the car.

When we arrived in Mikulash, my Uncle Geza, a well established veterinarian, met us in the railway station where we were reunited with Mother. After warm greetings and hugs, we walked to his new car while our mother hugged and kissed Pauline. But I saw that Mother and Pauline had retreated to a corner of the station and were arguing about something. When she returned, I asked, "Mama, what happened between you and Pauline?"

"She didn't want to take back the money she had given me for the furniture. I told her she had already helped us enough, just getting us safely here, but she wouldn't take it. Uncle Geza wanted her to at least take enough money for the train ticket back, but she wouldn't."

Then she looked down lovingly at us and brushed back my stiff hair with her hand. "You boys were very good," she said. "You did very well pretending not to know me and sticking to Pauline like that. I'm proud of you." She paused, "We are now safe, thanks to beautiful Pauline."

29

"What about *Apo*?" Ernst asked.

"I told him we were coming here. He will join us when he is finished working in the camp," she said.

But I understood the sad expression on her face which didn't match the confident sound of her words.

When France was invaded by Germany, all French citizens were expelled from Slovakia, sometimes forcibly.

* * * *

When I told this story to friends recently, I said, "We never saw Pauline again. She boarded the train and exited our lives, but her smiling face has remained with me forever. Isn't this the nature of angels? They appear when they are needed and then return to their own realm? And this one spoke French.

CHAPTER FIVE:
MIKULASH

Life was more normal in Mikulash. Although all Jews were required to wear the yellow stars, they were not as limited as they had been in Piestany. My brother and I went to the Jewish school and returned to the bedroom we shared in our grandmother's house where we played, studied, and slept. Some toys and books brought here during earlier vacation times were stored in an upright closet at the foot of our beds, and the window where we could watch the sunsets overlooked a green, lush meadow.

Rosalia tried to tell her new friends and old relatives what was happening to Jews in the west, but nobody believed her. I could tell by their faces that they thought she had gone a little strange after the disappearance of her husband.

"Your husband will return one day when he completes his duties in the labor camp and he won't find you there," one cousin objected. "Wouldn't you have been better to stay in Piestany?"

"You don't understand, it was a matter of life and death. I had to save my children. I regret to inform you that it will come here, too, and then you will understand and believe me."

Years earlier I had a friend in Mikulash, Anichka, a lovely girl, but older than I. She lived with her mother in the same courtyard as my grandmother, but she did not come to see me. I knew why.

I had often visited my grandmother during my school vacations. I would come, accompanied by my mother, who then left and came back to retrieve me, after a long two months of vacation. Or, at least they seemed long, as every time period seems when you are a child. I was seven years old when I first met Anichka. She was maybe 11 or 12. I met her in the inner yard of the apartment compound where my grandmother lived, close to the High Tatras in Slovakia.

Anichka, the daughter of my grandmother's neighbor, was very well liked by everybody in the compound. She was cheerful, pretty, and always ready to help. I remember her wheeling another neighbor who was confined to a wheel chair.

Since the first vacation I spent in Mikulash, she had become my friend, protector and mentor. In essence, she adopted me as her younger brother.   She had a particular affection for drama. Frequently, when our families met, she would create a curtain from a sheet, and instruct me behind it what to say in our play. When she opened "the curtain",we performed and everyone applauded with enthusiasm. In addition, our friendship extended beyond our dramatic performances. We used to go together to bath in a shallow bay of the Vah river, the main water artery of Slovakia, where I could wade in up to my knees and move around under her watchful eyes. I had utmost confidence that nothing bad could happen to me when she was around. This relationship continued for about three summers.

Then one spring day, I was surprised when my parents told me that Anichka was coming to visit me in Piestany, in western Slovakia. At that time, I attended grade 3 of the Jewish elementary school, and was known throughout the school as an excellent student. I had been reading since the age of four, books in both German and Slovak.
Anichka visited me at school. After we returned home and ate a hearty lunch that only my mother could prepare, we were allowed to visit the park. Anichka, being older, was, of course, in charge of security.

As we were walking through the narrow paths of the park, lined up by beautiful flowers, a question occurred to me. I stopped walking and looked in Anichka's eyes. "How come you are not at school?" I asked her, "since this is not vacation time? Or maybe it is in Mikulash?"

She was silent for a while and then lowered her eyes and answered me softly, almost whispering. "I am not at school anymore. I failed my grade and left school."

Perhaps it was my parental conditioning, which always caused me to study dilligently, that made me explode. "Oh shame on you, shame, shame! How can you be so ignorant?"

Anichka stood there silently with her bowed head, and then started to run, leaving me behind alone. When I came home by myself, I tried to salvage a relationship that had been so important to me. But when I tried to speak to Anichka, she did not respond. She turned away from me and ignored me.

My mother was quite puzzled by the events, and asked me, "What happened in the park? Why did Anichka come back crying?"

I did not feel I could tell my mother what happened. I felt ashamed and guilty. So I only shrugged my shoulders and retired into my room. When the door closed behind me, I also burst into tears. In the early afternoon my father took her to the train station and she returned to her home.

After prolonged mourning, I recovered with the hope that things would return to normal during my next visit to Mikulash. I wanted to forget that unfortunate conversation in the park and to continue as usual, as if it had never happened. But I was wrong. When I went to Mikulash the following summer, Anichka did not greet me. My grandmother told me that she was working, but afternoon and evening came and Anichka did not come to visit me. In fact, I hardly saw her that summer. When I glimpsed at her once on the stairs of her apartment, she merely waved to me lightly and disappeared inside. Anichka was no longer my close friend. As a matter of fact, she was no longer a friend of mine anymore. It was very hard for me to accept, but I continued to hope that one day she would appear in my grandmother's apartment. My hope was futile because it never happened. Mikulash without Anichka was not the same. The following year I spent the vacations in Ilava, at my paternal grandmother's place.

When we escaped Piestany and came again to Mikulash, our circumstances were very different. I saw Anichka maybe twice, but she did not talk to me. She was a young lady of 15 and had friends her own age. She was not interested in a 10 year old kid anymore, particularly after what had happened between us.

In Mikulash, I was once again enrolled in a Jewish school. All was well for a few months. I made several good friends, among whom was Yokko.

CHAPTER SIX:
SCHOOL AND MY FRIENDS

In 1943, Mikulash, which was called Liptovsky Svaty Mikulash, was a small calm city in central Slovakia with about 15,000 inhabitants, not far from the renown Tatra peaks, on the shores of the river Vah. It was surrounded by two or three dozen picturesque villages. In spite of the war raging around it, city life continued as more or less usual. The country of Slovakia had not yet been occupied directly by the Germans, although from time to time German officials appeared there. Slovakia had a puppet regime directed from far away Bratislava by a priest named Joseph Tiso. The local police were reinforced by the Hlinka Guard, who were supposed to deal with what was called the *Jewish Question* among other issues. Indeed, some Jews had been deported fom Mikulash to concentration camps in Poland, but many remained because they were considered "crucial to the Slovak economy." Others, like my little family, were there illegally.

In spite of occasional deportations, the Jewish community somehow functioned. There was a respectable synagogue and a functioning Jewish school with mixed grades from grade one to eight. The upper grades, from 4 to 8, had their own classroom and their own teacher. I was in grade five when I met Yokko Grossman, who was one grade lower.

The students hung out together, and often met in each other's houses or after school in the school yard, where there was an improvised football field. Sometimes we went for a walk to the nearby *hay* or forest or to the shores of the river Vah, unperturbed by the war around us and by the danger of being caught. Although we were actually aware of the dangers, we also sensed that the Hlinka Guard was not over-zealous in persecuting Jews. Actually, the Germans had to pay the Slovaks 500 marks as an extra incentive for every Jew deported,. This attitude varied from city to city, but in Mikulash the guardists were not very active in rounding up Jews, with the exception of two infamous men, Miklosh and Janichek, the leaders of the Guards. These two were, in the view of our adults, very dangerous, and quick to snatch any Jew whom they recognized in the street or outside the city borders.

I had many friends in my school and I liked my teacher. But I felt a special attachment to Yokko from our first encounter in the school. I liked to spend time in his company, discuss issues of common interest and plot all kinds of adventures. Later in my life I realized Yokko appealed to me because he was a small, chubby kid who always offered a welcoming smile, was an excellent listener and was a loyal friend. Our religious backgrounds were different. He came from an orthodox family, religiously observant, while I had a liberal background, influenced primarily by my uncle, the veterinarian. He had rejected Jewish observance as "immature.." However, he felt a strong passion for Zionism and Israel, where he emigrated after the war. Still, Yokko and I usually found common ground in our religious beliefs

I was a frequent visitor to the Grossman's house, and enjoyed their hospitality, kindness and warmth. Yet being kids, we spend much of our time in the street and in the nature surrounding Mikulash, not always completely aware of the dangers lurking at every corner.

One day Yokko and I ventured some five kilometers east of Mikulash to the village of Okolicne, which lay on the shore of the river Vah surrounded by fields of corn. As it was late into the summer, the stalks were really high, able to conceal kids of our age. In Okolicne, we noticed an assembly of people on the shore of Vah apparently celebrating something. As we watched, two black Mercedes cars drove up, and from them exited the infamous Miklosh and Janicek. It seemed to us at that moment that they were looking straight at us, and even calling us to approach. Maybe this was only a figment of our imagination, but we turned and ran into the corn fields with as much speed as we could. We ran and ran for some fifteen minutes before we dared to look back to discover that no one was chasing us. In the distance we heard Slovak folk music, and we felt finally safe.

When we reached Yokko's home, our chests heaved and we could hardly take a breath before we spilled the story, emphasizing our heroic escape from mortal danger. However, the response was not what we expected.

"Hmm," commented Yokko's father, "this is what you thought happened. You better stay close to home, because it can really happen."

Stunned by Yokko's father's disbelief in our adventure, Yokko accompanied me to my apartment. But our hope to receive a more admiring response vanished, when my mother dismissed our version, too.

"If it had been the head guardistas that spotted you, you would not be here now."

Disappointed and deeply offended by the reactions of our parents, we started to doubt the story ourselves, even though in our minds we were still able to see the chief guardistas pointing at us and calling us to approach them. So what was the truth?

All around us, political storm clouds began to gather. I noticed one day that some students didn't return to school after a weekend. When they didn't appear after several days, the teacher explained that they had been deported.

One day, a police car pulled up in front of the school. As I watched from my seat in the row nearest the window, two officers got out and marched into the school. They pushed open the door to my classroom, marched in, and literally yanked two boys out of their seats by their shirt collars. They dragged them outside and pushed them into the police car. That frightened me.

I reported the incident to my mother when I returned home from school. "Mama, two police guards came into our school and grabbed Shmuel and Abie today. Why would they do that?"

She only sighed and rolled her eyes to the ceiling. "Oh dear God," was all she said. She rose from her chair and walked down the stairs to her brother's veterinary office, entered it and closed the door.

I stared after her. I understood and did not wonder anymore. I knew. From my mother's face, from her deliberate silence as she descended the staircase and carefully, silently, closed the door behind her, I knew. Everything now began to come into focus.

And I worried. Now, day and night, I worried. What did it mean for me? For my brother? My mother? I also understood, too, that my father would never return. The ominous clouds in the sky that were the portent of storms had invaded the space behind my eyes. I couldn't see through them, but they were there, obscuring reverything else. I worried.

Slowly, other kids started disappearing from school. The word was that they all had been arrested and deported along with their families. The Nazi Hlinka Guard didn't do it as they had in Piestany, taking the men first. They took whole families who would just disappear in the evenings or at night.

CHAPTER SEVEN:
PERSONAL STORIES

A few days after Shmuel and Abie had been taken away, Miriam, a pretty eleven-year-old, approached me during school morning recess and shyly asked, "Otto, which girl in our school do you like the most?"

I thought for a while, then pointed to a petite, dark-haired girl. "Eva, that is the one I like the most. Eva."

"I like you the most," Miriam said, blushing a little as she gave me a quick kiss on the cheek and then ran back into the class. I only stared after her, saying nothing.

That afternoon, I stared out the window of my classroom too much, thinking not about the big tree outside with its scampering squirrel I loved to watch, but about Miriam's question.

42

What kind of fool am I. Here is a pretty, honest girl confessing her love for me and I didn't even respond. I didn't even say Thank You, or I like you a lot, too, or anything.

I began to consider how to rectify my unfortunate lapse. I knew where she lived, as I knew where all my classmates lived. So I decided I would surprise her later that evening by walking to her house to see her. There, I will tell her how nice it felt to have her ask me that, and to have her give me a little kiss. I will tell her that I really liked her a lot, and in fact, that I believed she was the prettiest girl in the school.

When the school bell rang signaling the close of studies, I put my books, paper and pencils inside my desk and shut the lid, put on my jacket and began the walk to her house, thinking of nothing but how good it would be to say what I had planned, how she would respond, maybe with another little kiss. And maybe I would give her a little kiss back and my words would all come out perfectly, just as I planned.

I walked for almost a mile on that cool May evening. It was dusk when I came to the corner nearest her house. When I turned right, I froze. Parked in front of her house was the infamous olive-green Hlinka Guard Razzia truck and Miriam's family was being herded into it as I stood watching. She saw me, smiled a wan smile, and waved almost apologetically as the rear gate of the truck was slammed shut, almost on her hand.

I shouted silently, *Miriam, where are you going? I have something important, really important to tell you.* But I was speaking only to myself. The truck revved its engine and roared away carrying my potential first love.

I stood, staring at the departing olive-green truck as it grew smaller and smaller and I felt my dream of making everything right with her fading into chalky dust under my feet. I walked a little further toward her house, drawn to see just a little bit more of Miriam, to understand a little better what I had just lost.

Could her whole family be one of those that were just disappearing, one after the other? What had they left behind?

Boldly, I walked up the stairs to her house, only intending to look into the window and see how she lived, but I could not resist trying the door knob. It turned easily under my nervous fingers.

I shouldn't be doing this. Once I had stepped into the foyer, I closed the door and could feel the intensity of the silence in a space that had, moments before, been filled with life, with her life, with the life of Miriam whom I might never see again.

That knowledge alone drove me back to the door and out into the street as fast as I could run. The very last thing I saw as I fled Miriam's house was the beautiful brass Menorah sitting on a lace doily on a table in the foyer. Miriam's mother had lit that every Friday night because that's what Jewish families do. And they had left it behind.

That night, I had hoped there was some mistake, that the truck was just taking them for questioning, that they would be returned and I would see her in her seat second row from the front two aisles over from him. But the next day, she didn't come to school. Her seat was empty. It took no imagination for me to unequivocally comprehend what had happened.

But what to do next? I wished my father were here. When I had told my mother about the two boys being yanked out of their seats and taken by the police, she had rolled her eyes and shut herself in her brother's office. This was a new situation that needed a father. He would know what to do. Obviously all Jews were in danger. I thought, *Not just danger. Life-threatening danger.*

The way my father had been shoved into the filthy train car, the way the boys had been kidnapped, the desperate last wave of Miriam before the door slammed, did not bode well for our futures. My mother and Ernest and I had been safe at my Uncle's house until now. But I wasn't so sure about the future.

We were fortunate. Another small, life-saving break was about to come our way. One may ask if any life-saving break can be small, but compared with what was about to happen, it may have been small but it was very important.

Rosalia, my brother and I were not registered as citizens of Mikulash. We had false papers identifying us as Slovaks from the very east of the country. The story we were said to tell if asked was that we escaped fearing the approaching Russian army. So we were not known as Jews. We had been living with Rosalia's mother and her brother Geza, but in January, 1943, Uncle Geza was transferred to Spishska Stara Ves, near the Polish border, and he took his mother with him. His was a protected profession because the Nazis had decreed that certain jobs were necessary to the war effort. As a veterinarian, he was needed to care for the horses in the German/Slovakian Army at their base in Stara Ves. So our little Rand family had an apartment all to ourselves in a building with eight other Jewish families. Rosalia and our next-door apartment neighbor, Hannah, had grown up together. She was a very close friend and the mother of Anichka.

One morning, Hannah appeared at our door. "Lenke," she said sounding frantic, "A German soldier . . ."

My mother interrupted, "A German?"

"Yes, not the Hlinka Guard, a real German soldier with SS on his shirt sleeve came to our door this morning and said all Jews in our building are summoned to a common outdoor meeting. He said we should take our bags because we will stay overnight in the Jewish synagogue. Then they will tell us where we are going. Oh Lenke, what are we going to do now?"

I heard the conversation and knew from what I had seen already that they were going to be hauled away in trucks.

My mother's face fell and she turned pale. I tugged at her dress sleeve. "Mama, we mustn't go there. We must leave here, but not go with them . . . " She brushed away my hand.

"Hannah, nobody came here to tell us. I wonder why?"

"I don't know, Lenke. Maybe you are just lucky. Maybe . . . I don't know."

She paused. "I guess I'd better go home and pack." She turned and walked across the hall.

"Hannah . . . . Hannah . . . " Rosalia called after her, but she did not respond. She didn't turn. She didn't look back.

Rosalia, almost as if on automatic pilot, turned and went to her bedroom where she began packing.

I followed. "Mama, listen to me. I am 11-years-old and I am the man around here now, and I have seen what is happening. I haven't told you everything because I know it worries you, but I watched Miriam's family being stuffed into a green Razzia truck and taken away, and she didn't come to school ever again. I saw those boys taken from our classroom. Jews are being taken and it doesn't look good for any of us. We must leave, but not go to the Synagogue for their meeting! They will take us away from there in those trucks!"

She didn't look at me. She just kept putting things in a suitcase.

I shouted. "Mama, listen to me! Do you hear me?" I had never shouted at my mother before. It was frightening.

"Otto, stop. I know you are trying to help, but there is nothing we can do. It is the whole police force of our country that has been taken over by the Germans. There is nothing we can do. Now go pack!"

I left and returned into my bedroom to think. Little Ernest was blithely working a puzzle. *At least he doesn't know what's going on.*

A few minutes later, to my amazement, I looked out his window and saw my mother approach the German soldier standing guard in the yard of the building. I opened the window and listened.

"You have not told us to gather with our friends at the Synagogue," my mother said, "and we wonder why. We are Jewish and we want to go with them."

"What's your name," the soldier asked.

"Rosalia Lea Rand."

"Rand, Rand, Rand," the soldier said, running his finger down a piece of paper.

"You are not on the list. You can't come. Go away! Don't bother me again." He threw his head back and straightened his back as if he were going to salute someone. Then he scowled at her, put the paper back in his pocket, turned his back to her and walked a few steps away from her.

Mother stood stock still for a moment. I stared, not believing our good fortune in the face of my mother's abominable request. *What was she doing? What on earth was she thinking, volunteering us to the Nazis?*

"We are not on the list?" I said aloud. "Why not? Maybe because we are not listed as citizens of Mikulash. But what a lucky break."

The Nazis obviously wanted some Jews, but why just a few at a time? To a child, this was just another piece of the puzzle in this terrifying and bewildering time. But I completely understood what a break we had just been handed by fate!

I soon heard her footsteps on the stairs and in the hallway. My mother said nothing to me as I stood in the doorway of my bedroom watching her. She walked to her bedroom where she began unpacking. Nothing more was ever said about the incident.

This virtually vacant building was our home for another several weeks. The only other remaining family, also Jewish, lived in an apartment upstairs. The father and grandfather were leather manufacturers, another protected profession. Now that all the other Jews were gone, and we Rands were obviously not registered as Jews, my brother and I could join the other children in a regular school. Our walking companion to school was the daughter of the leather-manufacturing family. Proximity prompts alliances. She wasn't my girlfriend, as Miriam might have become, but when I called her my best friend, she smiled.

Some other Jewish families remained in our neighborhood, sometimes for reasons even they themselves couldn't understand. Perhaps it had something to do with lists? The children of these families were mostly boys. We restless youngsters decided to form an impromptu Jewish defense group "to protect our families from the Nazis." We called ourselves "Partisans," and made leather belts and swords from remnants in the leather factory. That was the whole of our uniforms. Every day, after school, we occupied empty buildings or apartments and "fought" the Nazis to the death!

As the year progressed, life got more exciting for our little group of Partisans. Beginning with the chill of fall in 1943, an underground Jewish organization began smuggling

Polish Jews into Hungary, much as the Underground Railroad had operated in America during the Civil War. Slovakia became the transit corridor. Our apartment had three bedrooms. Two of them became hiding places for these Polish Jews in flight. Their visits were usually a week or so, and my friends and I became their guards. We played in the street in front of the building so we could spot any strangers walking by, spied on any neighbor who seemed too curious about our building, and we often sat by the window watching the street below after dark. When the visitors left, Rosalia made them food to take and one or two of our little Partisan group escorted them to their next stop, acting as if the men were their fathers or uncles just strolling to the drugstore for a lollipop. The local drugstore was usually the place of meeting with someone who would lead them further toward Hungary. The new contact would identify himself by wearing a small green scarf. Boys who stood watch outside could see them coming a block away! It was all very exciting to feel that they were part of the anti-Nazi underground.

I had begun to think of myself literally as a little man. Almost as tall as my mother, I felt a certain burden to help her avoid mistakes like the one she had made by asking the German if they could go along with the group of Jews who were being taken away. So the great question in my rapidly maturing mind, right after wondering how we would ultimately escape, was how my mother was getting the money to live on. She always seemed to have enough food, and left-over for the "visitors." One night after one of the groups had just been escorted to the local drugstore to meet a contact, I sat down on the couch and asked her.

"You know that my brother, your Uncle Geza, had done well financially," she began. "He told me before he left that he had invested money with a business partner of his, a builder here in town. Before he left, your Uncle Geza asked the builder to provide us with as much money as he could. When we need it, I just go there and ask, and he gives it to me. At least that is the plan. I have only used it once, but I will have to go again soon. Would you like to come? The requirement will be that you say nothing ever about this to anyone at all. This builder is not Jewish, and he is risking his life and business to help us. We have to be very careful to go there around dusk, and we have to be absolutely silent about our visits. Do you understand?"

Of course I did. Everything these days, I was sure, was a matter of life and death, or a great adventure, depending mostly on how old you felt you were at the moment.

The next evening at dusk, she took me and Ernest to see the builder. As we got closer and closer, I could see the fear in my mother's face. She was probably afraid of being betrayed, but there was nothing to do when she needed money but go there and ask for it. *When you are hungry*, I thought, *you gamble.*

The builder and his wife lived in a large, beautiful house surrounded by a lovely garden on the outskirts of town. I was astounded at how nice the two were. It had been a while since I had seen average people, not worried, not tense, and not Jewish, who lived the kind of life my family and I had lived before the Germans came. I was flooded with sad memories of what my family used to have, and at the same time, delighted to be in this house smelling the delicious meal the builder's wife had cooked. While we boys relaxed, my mother talked to the builder and his wife over cups of steaming tea poured from a lovely china teapot with a single rose painted on the side.

After dinner, even though chickens were very scarce, our hosts gave us three roasted chickens to take back to our apartment. What a treat since there were no longer chickens to buy anyplace in Mikulash. All the way home, my mouth watered just smelling the roasted chickens, my favorite, in spite of the fact that I was completely full from the scrumptious meal I had just eaten.

My mother returned to this builder many times and each time she was treated generously, given money, drinks and food. Clearly, my uncle had provided well for us and his friend was devoted, kind, and generous. How lucky we were!

Our situation remained stable until the summer of 1944. With the exception of some random searches, which our family was always warned about ahead of time by the Resistance, life was not unbearable. With forged papers, I became Otto Razicky instead of Otto Baruch Rand. Even so, Mother was afraid to let us go to school for fear of excessive exposure, so I read Jules Verne's science fiction and played soccer with some neighborhood boys all spring and summer, basically turning the war into a huge soccer fest. I had a map of the world left from my schooldays, and I avidly read whatever newspapers kept scores of whatever international games were still played.

Late in the summer of 1944, the builder told my mother and me during one of the money pick-ups that he was a member of the Slovak Resistance. He warned her that the fairly well-concealed Resistance was about to come out of hiding. When they did, equipped with weapons and ammunition parachuted down by the English and Free French pilots, they planned to take the Hlinka Guard by surprise. Eventually, Resistance Partisans conquered a number of cities and villages in central and eastern Slovakia, including Mikulash.

Daily, the sound of pounding cannons from the Russian front in the east was getting nearer and nearer. The builder said he was worried that instead of solving the German problem, the attacks could bring more Nazis and perhaps the worst of them, the SS. "If the partisans' resistance movement alarms the Germans," he said, "there could be hell to pay."

He had been right. The Germans mobilized massive numbers of troops in Slovakia, taking control of the "security" of the country along with the Hlinka Guard whom the Germans felt was not resolute enough to suit their ethnic cleansing visions. Soon, German troops were everywhere, and as far as they were concerned, there were no more "essential" and "non-essential" Jewish jobs. All Jews were targeted for death.

Even with the false birth certificates provided to us in Mikulash, Rosalia still did not feel her family was completely safe, so she moved us to a one-bedroom apartment in an area that was completely gentile. Soon even that was not completely safe. Razzia trucks drove the streets delivering soldiers who went door to door, searching for any remaining Jews. That time became known as "The Days of the Razzias." As Hitler began to visualize Germany's loss which predicted his end and the failure of his megalomaniacal vision for total control of the world, he accelerated his program to destroy the Jews. If he could only succeed at one thing, he wanted this to be it.

When The Days of the Razzias began along with Hitler's attempt to destroy all Jews, the underground found ways to warn Jewish families. My brother and I were taken by our mother on outings into a nearby forest. Not a cultivated park, but a real virgin forest with trails for hiking, mushrooms and herbs for picking, and secret caves where we had played Partisan. We loved these outings and were always sad to return home.

At the end of our third outing, before returning to our small apartment, Rosalia took us just half-way, stopping at a little railway switching station. I learned that Mr. Pozny, the head of the family who lived there and who ran the station, was the leader of the local Resistance. Unusual for that time, they had a telephone.

Rosalia told him she had a funny feeling that it would be dangerous to return home. "Could you please phone someone and ask?" she inquired.

Sure enough, the contact he phoned warned them that the Razzia raid was not yet over. We slept in the Pozny's barn that night.

We picked mushrooms and brought them to the Mr. Pozny's house, and his wife taught us which mushrooms were safe to eat and how to find them. We soon became experts on finding mushrooms. Mrs. Pozny also prepared a delicious mushroom stew and gave our family a big bag filled with with eggs and butter and all kinds of vegetables, enough for a week. The next morning, after another phone call, we walked back to our apartment.

At barely 12-years-old, one part of me still saw the whole thing as a big adventure - going to the forest, finding mushrooms and sleeping in the barn. My younger brother, who was aware of the danger but not scared, was just excited by the experience. I was older, however, and had begun to worry that this great escapade might not end well.

CHAPTER EIGHT:
ON THE RUN
BUNKERS, BRICKS, AND BETRAYAL

The Resistance underground communication system worked very well for several months. But finally, in late summer, 1944, word came that we could no longer stay in Mikulash because the Germans had further accelerated the killing of Jews. There were more house to house searches, and they were so unpredictable that escape into the forest for a day or two became impossible. We had to leave.

The Resistance directed our family to a village, Jalovec, about 10 km. north, just at the base of the beautifully rugged Carpathian Mountains. Religion in Slovakia was dominated by two very different groups, Catholics and Protestants. Catholics generally cooperated with the Germans which was very dangerous to Jews. The Protestants, however, openly preached against the Nazi regime on the basis that religious covenants forbade murder. They were determined to save as many Jews as they could, but they had to save them not only from the Germans, but also from the local Catholics who would have denounced them. It was a tightrope but our family had no choice. There were few places of refuge for Jews, especially places to which we could walk. We headed for Jalovec where the inhabitants were all Protestant.

Before we left, Rosalia visited the builder to get money and whatever food supplies she could carry. We dressed as peasants and walked with other peasants and their horses and cattle carts. Nobody paid us the least attention on our way.

A friendly peasant family had been notified of our arrival by the Resistance. They welcomed us with open arms and provided us with a lovely room with two soft beds , one for Rosalia, the other for us boys. A brook divided Jalovec in two parts, and on each side were decent and well maintained houses of the villagers. Each villager had a parcel of land for sowing wheat or barley and a stable for horses. Each family had cows which provided plenty of milk and cheese. Some farmers were wealthier than others but nobody was really poor. My brother and I attended the one classroom school there. Since I was the most advanced student, the teacher frequently left me in charge of the classroom and went to his farm to take care of his cows and poultry. Food in Jalovec was plentiful, but the diet caused problems for my mother.

One evening, not long after we arrived, the village had a ceremony to kill and roast a swine. While waiting for the creature to cook, the villagers sang and danced. Then they cut it up and invited us to eat. Rosalia, as a Jew, couldn't touch this forbidden food, but she couldn't tell anyone why because no one knew we were Jews. Our cover story had been that we were from eastern Slovakia and had fled the advancing communists from Ukraine. We boys had never eaten pork before, so it was just another adventure for always ravenous kids.

Everywhere we had walked, Rosalia lugged her large, heavy silver candlesticks used to light candles to commemorate Shabbat as Jews do every Friday night around the world. Our room was a bit isolated, situated at the end of a long corridor. Every Friday night, after making sure nobody was around, she lit the candles and said the Jewish blessings to celebrate the Sabbath. Then she had to go out into the dining room with the rest of the family and pretend to be grateful for their pork dinner which she usually vomited shortly after she ate.

It turned out that there were several Jewish families hiding in Jalovec. They used to meet late in the evening in a barn, where they had a large radio tuned to the Slovak version of BBC. This was a welcome occasion, especially when people learned that the Germans were losing the war.

But in spite of the German defeats, the Jewish families felt the noose tightening. There were more frequent raids every place the Germans suspected Jews might be hiding. The Resistance kept those in hiding informed, but their forces were strained to the limit managing both their guerilla battles against the Nazis and keeping the hidden Jews informed about the Razzia raids. So the thirty families hiding in various villages around Jalovec took their need for protective shelter into their own hands. Pooling their resources, they hired some friendly peasants build a bunker in a cave in the mountains. Camouflaged with trees and branches resembling a Jewish Sukkah, the entrance looked like the rest of the forest until one penetrated the opening itself. To get to the cave, the families had to climb the mountain on unmarked trails. Outfitted only for emergencies, the bunker was not intended for long-term occupancy. Only a few mattresses and blankets covered the floors. Although a few people had brought pillows and other supplies, nobody expected to spend more than a night or two there.

Then, about 4 AM one morning in October, our peasant host shook Rosalia awake. "The Resistance has notified everyone who is hiding here. The Germans are in the next village and on their way to Jalovec. You must leave and go up the mountain. You know where."

Rosalia woke up me and my brother, and put our coats on over our pajamas. We quickly put on our socks and shoes and ran up the mountain behind the house toward the bunker. She thought it would be overnight only, so she had brought no other clothes for us. But every day the Resistance warned us not to return, so we were all stuck in that cave for two weeks, totally dependent on the supplies and generosity of the other occupants. By the end of the second week, that generosity had been stressed to the maximum. We were all Jews in flight for our lives, but strains began developing among the cave dwellers.

One of the biggest problems was not food, it was education. The two groups of Jews who had congregated here were Western Jews and Eastern Jews. All agreed that the children should have Jewish studies, even in the bunker. However, the Eastern Jews, who had come from the areas close to Ukraine, wanted to educate their children in Yiddish. The Western Jews wanted them to learn in German or Slovak. The Eastern Jews prevailed because they had a teacher living in the bunker. This angered my mother who was a Western Jew.

Shortly after the decision to teach the children in Yiddish, Janek arrived. He was a young resistance worker who had functioned for some time as the liaison between the builder friend of our Uncle Geza and my mother. He had tracked us to the bunker to find out whether they needed more money.

"Janek, you can't imagine how glad we are to see you," Rosalia said, uncharacteristically hugging him. "I'm not respected here at all. These people want to teach our children in Yiddish, a language they will never be able to use in the world to gain employment. I must leave here. Do you know of any alternate place where we could hide?"

As she talked, I could see Janek looking her over with great sympathy. My formerly quite elegant and beautiful mother was wearing a ragged nightgown partially covered by an old coat that had seen better years. Her hair had obviously not been washed for a while, and her face was pale, drawn and haggard. As the wife of a beauty salon owner, she had formerly owned lovely cosmetics and her hair had been impeccable. Now, it hung in tangled strings like a discarded fishnet.

Janek thought for a few moments. "There is a bricklayer back in Mikulas who lives on the huge grounds of the brick factory. They have lots of housing for employees who come and go, so he believes the Germans will not pay much attention to anything as long as the bricks come out of the factory on time. He has offered to help house some Jews. I can take you there now if you wish, and I have money for you. There aren't any Germans around. They are all tied up about 10 kilometers north of here where there is a Resistance insurrection. We have to stage those sometimes to get them away from critical areas so we can move people. So here I am. Let's go."

The timing was fortunate. Temperatures were above freezing during our hike down the mountain, which was unusual for November. On the way through Jalovec, we stopped at the home of our hosts to clean up a bit, change into our normal clothes, and pick up Rosalia's large carrying valise with the precious candlesticks, and a few other belongings. The village had not yet been occupied full-time by the Nazis. They had just cleared out any Jews and then left, so our family was lucky in two ways. We managed to be away from Jalovec, hiding in the bunker when the Nazis checked every single house. And we managed to leave the bunker just ahead of a

Nazi raid. Several days later, Janek told us that the Nazis had found the bunker and had taken away everyone, loading them onto the infamous olive-green Razzia trucks. Except for the time she had tried to talk the German soldier in front of their building into letting us go with other Jewish friends, my mother's instincts were almost unerring. *If only my father had listened,* I thought.

At the time, Rosalia was 35 years old, strong and healthy, and a very good looking woman. She was also a tireless walker. People noticed her, which was a problem at times. The 10 kilometer. walk back to Mikulash was as uneventful as the original journey had been. Everyone had been right when they said the Germans ignored the peasants and their trail of animals. When the Germans passed, they rudely forced the peasants to move down into the barrow pits alongside the road.

Janek's friend, the bricklayer was a tall, strong, handsome man of about 45. His wife was younger, but she was almost never there. She frequented the taverns in town and often came back quite drunk. They had no children but in the bricklayer compound, there were many children, although my brother and I were not allowed to mix with them. Instead, we took some bricks and built ourselves a fortress where we could hide in case the Nazis arrived. We also found a frozen pond a short distance down the hill. We made an opening in the ice at the edge of the pond where the ice had crept higher onto the ground, above the water's edge. We dug into the earth, making a small cave that was pleasant and warm with a roof of ice. We stashed three blankets taken from the bricklayer's home in our ice cave, our alternate hiding place in case of emergency.

One day, playing in our brick fortress, we heard shouting from outside.

"Look, look. It's falling. It's falling. It's on fire." Everyone was shouting the same words and staring at the sky as the group ran toward the banks of the River Vah.

We boys joined the running crowd, not thinking, in the heat of the excitement, to ask permission from our mother. Excited people had gathered on one bank of the river, to watch a flaming plane diving nose-first before it crashed into the earth on top of a hill just beyond the opposite river bank. Moments later, the crowd could see a parachute falling slowly toward them. As the American pilot, a black man, landed on the other side of the river, clamored to his feet, and shed his parachute, the people pointed him toward the villages behind the forest held by the Resistance. We boys could hear nothing, but what was happening was obvious to everyone, including Germans who had seen it from afar.

Soon German trucks came roaring over the bridge across the Vah. Soldiers jumped out and ran into the crowd. From the people pointing the other direction, I could see that the villagers were misleading the Germans about the direction the pilot had taken to escape. My brother and I silently cheered twice. First, because the pilot had escaped and the Germans were hotfooting it in the wrong direction. Second, because it was the first time we had seen a black man and here he was, an American hero, a pilot!

CHAPTER NINE:
MAZULINA

I reflected on our many fortunate, seemingly miraculous, experiences.

If the French woman, Pauline, had not pretended we were her children on the train, we might have been taken off the train and sent away. If the Guard had not refused Mother's request to join the other Jews in Mikulash, we would have been arrested and taken to a concentration camp. If I had not been awake and had not heard the footsteps on that bitterly cold, snowy night, the French Partisans would have passed, never knowing my family was there. If they had not had cognac and used it to awaken my mother and Ernest, we would have frozen to death there in the snow. If we had not reached the gazebo and seen the house beyond it by some miracle in the early morning fog when we were nearly dead with exhaustion, we might have wandered on the mountain until we died.

Once we had finally arrived in Maluzina, we had been taken in by the forester and his wife after our harrowing hike through the snow and trackless wilderness, or we would surely have perished. But our troubled life continued. After we had reached that friendly home and had been fed and thawed out a little, minus a few frozen toes, our lives, I decided, had been saved by a series of small miracles. I continued to hope for at least one more.

"Where can we go to stay?" I piped up when the forester said we couldn't stay at his house. "There must be somebody here who could let us stay with them for a few days. You said it is a miracle that we made it over the mountain at night in this cold, so I guess we are not supposed to die. Surely somebody has space for us." My logical optimism had made them all laugh in spite of the fearful chill that had arrived with the Nazi victory the night before and had which nothing to do with temperature.

"I will call the Mayor and ask him where you can stay," the forester had replied, ruffling my hair.

A few hours later, the Mayor himself arrived. The forester had covered my mother and Ernest in blankets and put them in the back of his sleigh. The Mayor rode with him in the driver's seat. I walked alongside. So many Ukrainians were clearing away their wounded and dead that nobody paid any attention to us.

"It's actually not safe in Maluzina anymore either," the mayor said darkly, "but I guess you people can't go any further, so I will place you with Veronika."

We were escorted to the one-room shack of a completely deaf old woman who was in charge of the village bull. The village had one bull for all the cows, and she was its caretaker. It was a job she could do to repay the Mayor for his care of her. The village depended on that precious bull for all the calves. After the Mayor left us there, he warned us to stay inside and not to go outside that house for any reason!

"You are not the only Jews here," he said sternly. "There are quite a number hiding in this village, and we have to be very careful because the Nazis will destroy the whole village if they discover any of you. You must be very quiet, and if anyone walks by, get out of the view from the window. We will make sure you have food delivered."

Our mother had thanked him profusely, assuring him that her boys would be quiet as mice. Unfortunately, a few days later, Ernest's toes had become so infected that he cried out in pain all night. Veronika couldn't hear anyway, so all communication had to be done with a rudimentary sign language. She understood clearly from the Mayor that she had to hide our little family, so she made sure they were completely out of sight when she opened the door to go take care of the bull.

At night, I curled up in an opening in the wall above the clay stove that provided heating for the hut as well as a cooking surface while my mother and Ernest slept on a floor mat. The advantage of my sleeping place was its warmth. The disadvantage was that it was filled with lice. They loved my hair, but even the crawling lice didn't keep me from sleeping soundly night after night because of my accumulated exhaustion.

During our first few days in the tiny village of Maluzina, the shooting never stopped. On the third night that we were there, the war came to our porch. The partisans had been hiding in the forest, waiting to chase out the Ukrainian Nazis. I could see the situation was not only dangerous, but complex.

"How does it work," I had asked the forester as we all waited for the Mayor that first day. "The Russians are coming our direction and they are very close. The Ukrainians are fighting on the side of the Germans, but they are actually Russians, so aren't they traitors to their own country?"

"You understand it very well for one so young," he replied. "We thought that when the Russians got very close, the Ukrainians would give up and run. We never dreamed they would come back here and take our village again!" I could tell he was completely disgusted, even more than afraid by the whole confusing mess.

I asked him, "Do the Russians like you? Your village, I mean?"

"As far as we know they are just fighting the Germans, not anyone else.".

I thought for a while. "So I guess things will improve when the Russians get here," I speculated.

The forester chuckled. "With God's blessing," he said. "With God's blessing."

The fierce battle outside their hut that third night was terrifying, perhaps the most lethal threat the partisans had yet encountered. Bullets flew through the walls of the thin little shack as we all huddled against one side wall wrapped in blankets. One of the bullets hit Veronika's cat, killing it. Through all the violent fighting outside, the deaf old woman slept.

There are, I thought, *some benefits to being without hearing.*

At daylight, the Mayor proudly announced from his front porch that the resistance had chased out the Nazis.

The announcement was premature. At nightfall, the Ukrainian Nazis returned with reinforcement, chasing the partisans back into the forest. Fortunately this time the gun battle occurred at the other end of the village.

In addition to the return of the Nazis, our family had two other problems. First, the food had run out, and we had nothing to eat. Despite the stern warning from the Mayor, Rosalia had to send me out for food. The Mayor's home, three doors down, was also the town grocery store. When I had returned safely, my mother told me the second piece of bad news:

"Otto, I am out of money. That was the last of it." She looked at me as if I were a grown man, which often, these days, I felt I was.

"Mama, if it weren't for this silly shooting, I could try to do some work, but I'm not sure what I can do in this situation."

"I know what we must do," she said. "Do you remember Mr. Pozonoy from the switching station? I heard from the forester's wife that he is hiding in the next village about two kilometers. east of here. We need to see if we can find him and ask if he could lend us some money until we can get it from the builder."

We? I thought. *She means me.* "Do you want me to go there, Mother?" I asked.

"Otto, I can't walk with these infected toes. It is up to you."

Once again, I had to violate commands. Although I was not supposed to stick my nose out the door, much less go walking around between villages, I could see this was an emergency. And, at almost 13, I was nearing manhood. If life were normal, I would be preparing at the Synagogue for my Bar Mitzvah, the official commemoration of the metamorphosis from boy to man in the Jewish culture. Now, it became my manly duty to save my family.

Many military vehicles passed him, but there was no shooting. A village boy walking down the road was invisible, like bushes beside the road. When I arrived in the next village, it was relatively easy to locate the Pozny family. They were amazed to see me and even more astonished to hear the long tale of our miraculous escapes. I finally explained the purpose of my daring visit. "We are out of money."

The minute I said those words, Mr. Pozny reached into his pocket and handed me 200 Crowns, today's equivalent of about 60 U. S. dollars, which was an enormous sum at that time. Before I left, Mrs. Pozny fed me a huge meal with the family and she packed food for me to take back to my mother, Ernest and Veronika. As I walked back in the early dusk of February, I marveled again at how kind people had been to my family through our ordeal. Angels and human kindness were the two secrets of our survival, both of them puzzling in their own way and often having a delicate counter-balance to the evil I had seen every day for three years. On my walk back, I plumbed philosophical depths I thought I might have encountered in my Bar Mitzvah studies. *Perhaps,* I thought, *this was just a different way of becoming a man.*

When I returned, Veronika was cooking a pig foot in gelatin. I went to the Mayor's store once more and bought poppy seeds and noodles which my mother, hobbling around on one foot, cooked for us. Even with her handicap, she was able to wash our clothing and now that she had money again, to buy food and cook our meals. She did not eat pig's feet.

Our third major problem was not my head, and or the rest of my body, which never stopped itching from the lice. It was Ernest's gangrenous toes. Mother had been changing the bandages daily, but his toes were now swelling with accumulated puss and his temperature was rising. He needed medical care desperately but the only doctor was in the Ukrainian Nazi unit. My mother insisted to the Mayor that, no matter what, we had to bring the doctor to Ernest to save his life.

"If we don't, he will die. He has now a fever and it is getting higher. He screams all night with the pain. We have no choice," she said firmly.

"You understand that you are endangering not only your family, but our entire village since that has been sheltering you," the Mayor said, hesitating.

"I'm sorry. I'm willing to take my chances to save the life of my son. We have not come this far and gone through this much for me to just watch him die of these frostbitten toes," she said even more firmly. "Perhaps the doctor will not know we are Jews. You can just say we are running from the Communists."

My poor brother was in agony. My mother was beside herself with worry. "If I could just get my hands on a gun, I would kill Hitler," Ernest screamed.

A short while later, the Mayor returned with the doctor who treated Ernest for three days, sprinkling a yellow powder on his toes and giving him other medicines. It was now late February. The Russian Army was only 50 km. away, according to the Mayor. The evening of the third day, the doctor returned to his camp and reported to his commander that Ernest was Jewish. The doctor had seen that Ernest was circumcised when Ernest had undressed.

The Ukrainian Commander and two of his lieutenants burst into Veronika's cabin, their guns pointed at the our little family. Behind them, the Mayor and about twenty villagers approached, and as a group, pushed in to position themselves between the armed soldiers and our family.

"You were hiding Jews here," the Ukrainian Commander shouted at the Mayor: "We are taking them out to shoot them."

"You can't do that. They are sick. They are not dangerous. They are not going to endanger the German Empire," the Mayor replied firmly.

"No, you must bring them out. I am going to shoot them now. Those are my orders and I must do it right now."

My mother started to walk out the door, looking resigned but not frightened. She was willing to face her death. She had never known how her life would end, but obviously we had run out of miracles. I could see in her face that she had made up her mind to be courageous.

Then the Mayor spoke again with even more force in his voice: "Before you kill them, you will have to kill all of us, including me. We will not let an innocent family be murdered for no reason, no matter what your orders say."

The Commander hesitated, clearly puzzled. "Why is a crowd of ordinary villagers protecting a Jewish family? Why would you do that? Do you people see more in these Jews than I have been lead to believe?"

He knew the Russians were almost in the village and he was about to have to flee for his own life. "If we lose this race to save our lives," he said to his subordinate, "what would our Orthodox religion say about our having killed an innocent mother and her two children because they were Jews. I always thought there was good reason to get rid of them, but these villagers are just simple people like our own families."

He turned, and made a dismissive motion with his right hand which I have never forgot, and said, "Well, if this human shit lived until now, let them die in their own shit." And he and his lieutenants walked away.

The next morning, there was not a single Ukrainian Nazi left in the camp at the edge of the village. This time, it wasn't a partisan victory. They had fled ahead of the oncoming Russian Army.

Apparently, some Slovaks were angels, also.

CHAPTER TEN:
THE LIBERATION

"The Russians are coming, the Russians are coming," the village boys ran shouting. Shortly after, they shouted, "The Russians are here!"

They clamored up onto the slowly rolling green monsters that barely halted for them. Russian tanks officially captured the village at noon. The soldiers of the Russian Army, marching tall and proud, entered the village singing something I assumed was a Russian victory song. Everyone was screaming with joy. Tears rolled down women's cheeks as their men hugged them. Families stood in great clutched pods, their children squeezed tightly, all crying, unable to show their enormous relief any other way as the soldiers marched on through the town and out the other side.

Finally, a power they could feel had arrived to counter the German nightmare of the previous four years. Not just Partisan firepower, I thought, but the power of victory of one enormous country over the forces of evil in another. I was twelve years old and this was a kind of evil incomprehensible to a 12-year-old, an evil that had tried to kill every Jew for no reason I could imagine and from which, time after time, we had barely escaped. For years after, I tried to describe the momentous events of that day as I saw them, but I could never quite say enough. I could never make it sound as good as I had felt inside.

"Mama, mama," I shouted, breathless, as I ran into Veronika's cabin. "The war is over, the war is over! We are safe!"

Veronika turned to me as though her deafness had vanished and asked, "What did you say, boy? Don't yell, just say it."

I joined the celebration outside. One of the Russian officers with a lot of brass trim on his jacket approached me, stuck out his hand, and said in Russian, "Who are you, young man?"

I guessed at what he asked from his tone. "I am a partisan," I replied, shaking the man's hand proudly.

The officer laughed a jolly, hearty laugh, throwing his head back. Then he handed me a sausage, of which the Russians seemed to have an endless supply.

"Thank you, sir, but wait! I need your help," I said quickly in Slovak before he could walk on by. "My mother and brother are in terrible trouble. We hiked over the mountain at night, running from the Germans, and their toes are frostbitten and infected. They need a doctor. Could you help?" Because Slovak and Russian are related languages, he seemed to understand me. Immediately, the officer, who obviously was a commander, waved his arm and a soldier came running. "See to it that this boy's mother and brother are treated immediately at our field hospital. Run!" The soldier saluted and ran toward the white van with a Red Cross on the side that had followed the troops in. Within minutes, following my directions, the van arrived at the cabin door. A doctor entered, checked my mother and brother, wrapped them in blankets, put them on stretchers and loaded them in the van.

The commander, with two or three other soldiers, had waited outside with me. Before the van pulled away, after consulting with a doctor, he said, "Don't worry. Your mother and brother are being taken to our field hospital. They will probably have to have their toes amputated and that requires emergency surgery, but we know how to do that. They will be fine."

Meanwhile, the soldiers took me into one of the tents they were setting up at our end of the village. Laughing and joking with me, they called me "The Little Partisan," and handed me a new watch - a reward, they said, for his brave fighting. Little did they know!

Two days later, my mother, who had lost two toes, and my little brother, who came close to losing his life in addition to all the toes on one foot, were transferred to a civilian hospital in Poprad, Slovakia, two hours east. I sat beside the driver and went with them in a special Russian Command Ambulance along with two soldiers who had become fond of me, always addressing me as "The Little Partisan."

They left me with my mother and brother at the hospital. With no room for me to sleep beside them, I was bedded down in the almost empty, locked psychiatric ward.

"I can't sleep there again," I told a nurse the next morning. "It gives me the creeps, and I hate not being able to get out to go to the bathroom."

"I'm sorry, son," she said, not unkindly, "But we have no other space. This is it!"

"Well then," I announced, "I think I will go and try to find something on my own."

Heading back to the Russian camp, I encountered a soldier who knew me and I asked him if he knew whether there were any surviving Jewish families in Poprad.

"I have no idea, but you are completely safe to go ask that in the town. Good luck," he said as he handed me another watch. I wondered if these watches had these been taken off dead bodies?

It was the end of February and the rivers had started to thaw. As I walked across the bridge from the hospital into town, I saw bodies of horses and dead soldiers floating on the melting ice. Nobody could distinguish between German, Russian, Slovak or Ukrainian corpses. *How silly war is*, I thought. *In the end, in some way, it destroys everyone it touches.*

A few inquiries yielded the name of a Jewish family, the Herzogs, who had just returned to their own quite luxurious apartment from hiding. They not only housed me with them and fed me sumptuous meals, they sent food with me to my mother and brother every day.

"Mama," I asked one day about two weeks into my mother's hospital stay, speaking in my newly emerging deeper voice, "we are fine here for the moment, but what is our long-term destiny?"

"We have to locate Uncle Geza," she replied. "We know that he was moved to Stara Ves about 350 kilometers north of here. But we don't know whether he's alive. He was protected until the Germans came, but maybe not after that. We just don't know." She stopped. "Oh, Otto, I feel so helpless here with this infected foot. It's healing, but it's so slow! And I still worry a lot about Ernest, that he might lose his foot." She winced, throwing her head back against the brass bedstead and breathing heavily through her mouth as if she might cry.

"Don't worry, Mama, I'll find Uncle Geza. You just stay here and get well and watch out for Ernest. There is a soldier outside the hospital who knows me. I will tell him also to look after you, and I am sure the Herzog family where I am staying will continue to bring you food. You will be okay. I will be back soon." Without waiting for a response, I kissed her and left, feeling the very adult responsibility of caring for my family until my father returned.

I spoke to my Russian soldier friend outside the door. By then, I was able to speak Russian quite well. The following day, I was on my way to Stara Ves on a Russian troop truck with another group of Russian soldiers who laughed and teasingly called me "The Little Partisan."

Between Stara Ves and Poprad were high mountains. The Russians had to leave me at the foot of the nearest mountain over which was Stara Ves. From there, only horse-drawn peasant carts could access the other side. I climbed onto the back of cart, and as I left, the Russians handed me a huge bag of sausages. It did not matter to me that they were pork. I shared them with the cart-driver. It was all we had to eat.

After one day, one night, and half of a second day, I arrived in Stara Ves and found the house locals described to me. My uncle was again the town veterinarian and was overjoyed to see me alive!

"Otto, Otto, my darling Otto," he said, squeezing me so tightly I could barely breathe. "Why are you here by yourself? Where is your mother? And Ernest? Are you hungry? Are you thirsty? Come in . . . . tell me everything!"

The story took a while. When I described how my mother had given us the Jewish equivalent of last rites, my Uncle Geza cried. When I got to the joy of the Russian conquest and the arrival of the ambulance, he said only, "Praised be God." Then, moments later, "I only hope the salvation we feel now from the Russians lasts and does not turn into a Russian occupational dictatorship."

"Now," he continued, "my heroic young man. You can relax a little. I will send a car to pick up your mother and brother."

"They can't leave yet. The infection is still in their feet," I said. "But I need to go back and tell them the good news. Before I leave, we must set up some sort of communication system so I can let you know when to send the car." My new Russian soldier friends filled the gap, agreeing to become the communicators.

After crossing the mountain again in another peasant cart, I hitched a ride on one Russian truck and then another. Wherever the soldiers slept, I slept with them. Usually, they drove into a village and asked to stay in the homes of locals.

They were not very well liked because they were stealing, particularly watches. Every soldier had five or six on his arm. But I considered them saviors.

I arrived back at the hospital a few days later to find my mother healed enough that the bandages up to her thigh had been removed, leaving only her foot wrapped. She was able to walk on crutches. Added to that accomplishment was her joy and relief at hearing that her brother was alive and planned to send for us all.

"Otto," my mother said a day or two before her release from the hospital, "we must return to Mikulash, not go straight to Uncle Geza's house. If your father is alive, that is where he will come. And I must get my candlesticks and clothes, especially my winter warm coat and sweaters from the bricklayer's house."

In early July, we took the train from Poprad to Mikulash. The bricklayer's wife was no more pleasant than she had ever been when we picked up our belongings, but the bricklayer himself had been promoted to a managerial position. He still wanted to come with Rosalia to Piestany. Again my mother declined, saying that she was waiting for her husband to return. She never stopped waiting until years later when she found out from a survivor from Auschwitz that my father had been murdered.

Mr. Pozny of the train switching station had become Mayor of Mikulas because the Resistance formed the governments after liberation. After visiting the Pozonys and thanking them, we went to find the builder. His house was still there.

His wife who was still there told us, "He was taken by the Nazis because they found out he was not only in the Resistance, but was also a Communist. I don't know what has happened to him, and I fear the worst. Every day I pray that he will return," she said.

Her once cheery and helpful demeanor had vanished along with her husband. It greatly saddened me and my mother that this kind, gentle and helpful man who had saved our lives had now probably lost his own.

After teaching myself everything I could during the war years, I returned to high school. My troubles with being Jewish weren't life threatening anymore, but they weren't over either.

My high school chemistry teacher repeatedly said, "Too many Jews are still here. Too many are alive. The Germans didn't do a very good job."

Before the war, Piestany had a Jewish population of 2,500. Now only 200 remained, but even this was too many for him. I had several friends and one of them was very connected to the Communist Central Bureau.

I told my mother what the teacher had said. "Mama, I'm going to report this. It is not right."

"No, please Otto, don't do it. Don't make waves. We will suffer from it, and we've had enough suffering." She even brought a leader of the Jewish community to try to dissuade me.

I insisted. "No, Mama, I couldn't protest the terrible injustice during the war, and now I'm not going to be quiet. What's not right is not right. We can't let the Germans win now after the whole world fought a war to defeat them!"

I went with a friend, a Gentile, to the Communist headquarters. The team that they sent to investigate interviewed many students, including the principal and other teachers. They demoted the offending teacher to the position of assistant teacher and sent him to a distant small village.

I was not there to share the victory. My mother's sister, who had survived Auschwitz, emigrated to Israel in August, 1949, along with their brother, my Uncle Geza, and his family.

EPILOGUE

The war officially came to an end on May 5, 1945, with the formal surrender of the Germans to the American General, Dwight Eisenhower. The world breathed a sigh of relief, but I never stopped wondering why it all had to happen in the first place. What sort of insanity grips people and causes this sort of world-wide mayhem? Today, at 85, I am still asking that question.

Now when I am asked to reflect on our experiences, I say, "Sometimes you meet people who are very decent and helpful, and during that terrible time, we met a lot of them. Were we lucky? Maybe, but maybe the truth is that most people are decent and helpful and somehow they get overshadowed in our memories by the evil ones."

Why were the Russian soldiers in Slovakia kind to Jews when Russians, under Stalin, were brutal to them in other areas of Russia? I am not sure.

I'm just sure they were kind to me, calling me "The Little Partisan." I never identified myself to them as a Jew, only as a partisan, probably to my benefit. They must have known we were Jews because we had been in hiding and because of my search for the Herzogs in Poprad. But perhaps they considered us special Jews worthy of their protection. I don't know.

Even in Russian-occupied Stara Ves, my Russian soldier friends would come as a group to Uncle Geza's house because my aunt, his wife, made very good borscht. They sat with us, ate with us, sang and danced with us, and they were always a very friendly people.

My friendship had an additional benefit. I learned Russian from the soldiers and when schools reopened in what became the United Czechoslovakia, all students were required to learn Russian.

I learned a few more languages during my years in Israel where I lived in a youth *aliyah* with a group of Dutch and Czech Jews who had escaped the Holocaust. In addition, of course, I learned Hebrew.

I took the name Baruch, and my brother Ernest took the name David. We both became ardent Israelis, eventually serving in the Israeli Army. When I was released, I enrolled at Hebrew University in Judaic studies and Biblical archaeology, becoming a Judaic Scholar. I still take delight teaching Torah classes.

In spite of the fact that Ernest had lost all the toes on one foot, he was admitted into the Israeli Army. After being fitted with special orthopedic shoes, he rose to the position of Colonel in the Israeli Air Force. He walked and ran as if he still had all his toes.

After earning my Master's degree, I searched for a country in which to teach for one year and went to Ecuador, where I lead Jewish youth and taught Near-Eastern history at the University of Quito. There I met my wife, a Jewish student who had been born in China. When the Communists took over, her father had been fined several million dollars and jailed as a capitalist for 13 months. When he was released, the family had emigrated to Ecuador.

After two years in South America, I moved to Chicago, Illinois in 1961, where I enrolled at the University of Chicago. After studying there for one year, I finally finished my education at the University of Toronto. In Toronto I founded a Jewish school which became well known and which I operated for most of my life until I moved to Mexico and settled in the village of Ajijic in the state of Jalisco.

My mother, Rosalia Leah Rand, remained a strong and determined woman until she died in Israel at the age of 92.

Manufactured by Amazon.ca
Bolton, ON